# A Bible Alphabet Activity Book

**Alison Brown**

THE BANNER OF TRUTH TRUST

THE BANNER OF TRUTH TRUST
3 Murrayfield Road, Edinburgh EH12 6EL, UK
P.O. Box 621, Carlisle, PA 17013, USA

*

© Alison Brown 2007

*

ISBN-13: 978 0 85151 964 7

*

Typeset in Comic Sans at the
Banner of Truth Trust,
Edinburgh

Printed in the U.S.A by
Versa Press Inc.,
East Peoria, IL

Introducing little children to well known Bible stories

For Barbara,
and others like her,
who love to teach little
children about God.

# aaaaaaaaa

ark

God told Noah to build an .................
All the animals and people who would go inside
it would be safe.

# bbbbbbbbb

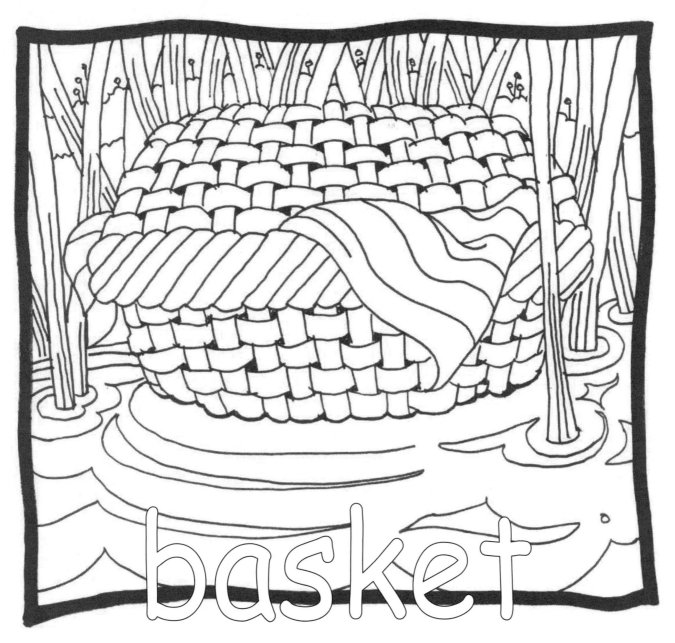

basket

Baby Moses slept in a bulrush ..........................
His mother didn't want the wicked king to find him.

CCCCCCC

coat

Joseph wore a lovely colourful ...................
No-one else had a coat quite like it!  It was
very special.

# dddddddd

# donkey

Balaam got a shock when his ..................... spoke!

# eeeeeeeee

earth

God made our wonderful .........................
He made it just right for people to live in!

f f f f f f f f

fish

Jonah was swallowed by a great big
...................... Three days later it coughed him
safely out on the shore!

# ggggggggg

giant

Goliath was an angry ........................
God helped David the shepherd boy to bring
him tumbling to the ground.

# hhhhhhhhh

## house

Martha liked to clean the ................ and cook tasty meals.  Mary liked listening to Jesus.

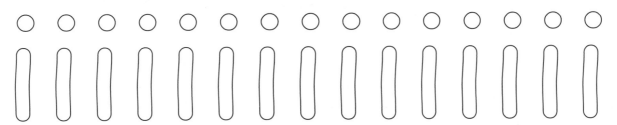

Paul used lots of ............... He wrote many letters to his Christian friends. He taught them wonderful things about God.

JJJJJJJJJJ

jail

Peter was put in ...................., even though he hadn't done anything wrong. God sent an angel into the jail to help him.

# kkkkkkkk

king

King Solomon was a very wise ....................
He asked God to help him make good rules.

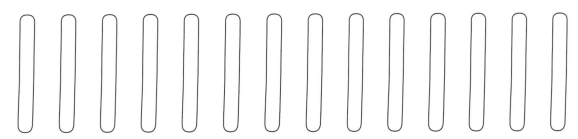

Daniel was thrown into a pit with some hungry
...................... God took care of Daniel. Not
one of the lions touched him!

# mmmmmmmm

# manger

Mary's baby had to sleep on the hay in a
............................... His name was Jesus and
he was the Son of God.

# nnnnnnnn

needle

Dorcas enjoyed sewing with her ..................
She was good at making clothes.  She made
lovely coats for all her friends.

OOOOOOOO

oil

Elisha saw God work a miracle with a little jar of ................. When the oil was poured out it filled all the big jars!

ppppppppp

picnic

A little boy gave his ..................... to Jesus.
Jesus used the five loaves and two fish to
feed thousands of hungry people!

qqqqqqqqq ppppppppp

queen

Jezebel was a wicked ...........................
God saw everything she did and he was very
angry.

# rrrrrrrrrr

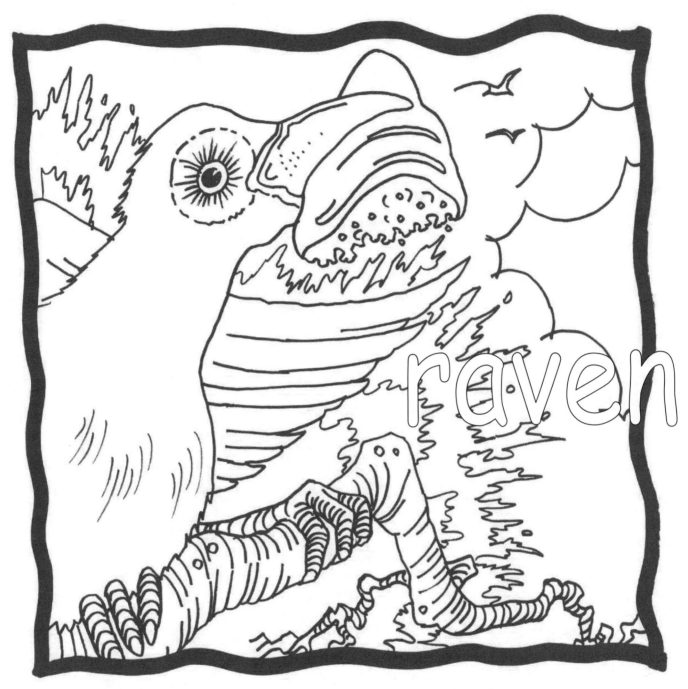

raven

God sent some ...................... to feed Elijah.
Twice every day they brought bread and
meat and dropped it just beside him!

# SSSSSSSSS

shepherd

Jesus says that he is the Good ....................
and we are the sheep.  He loved the sheep so
much he was willing to die for them.

† † † † † † † † † †

tent

Abraham lived in a ................., while he was travelling. He was going to the new land God had promised to give his family.

# UUUUUUUUUUU

## unleavened bread

Sometimes God's people ate ............................... ...................... They ate it when they were thanking God for having helped them.

# VVVVVVVV

vineyard

Naboth owned a lovely ...........................
Big juicy purple grapes grew on the vines.
King Ahab wished it belonged to him!

# WWWWWW

wall

The ................ around the city of Jerusalem was broken down. Nehemiah asked all the people to help him fix it.

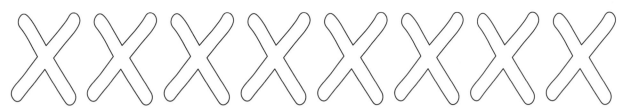

Aaron often saw the special golden ................
that was kept in God's house.  Inside it there
was a copy of God's laws.

# Yyyyyyyyy

yoke

Job was a rich man.  He had five hundred
........................ of oxen.  Job was able to praise
God, even when things went wrong.

# ZZZZZZZZ

Zion

Heaven is often called ........................... We read in the Bible that Jesus, the Son of God, will be the light in heaven!

# You can look in your Bible to find out more:

| | |
|---|---|
| ark | Genesis chapter 6, verses 13–22 |
| basket | Exodus chapter 2, verses 1–10 |
| coat | Genesis chapter 37, verses 3–4 |
| donkey | Numbers chapter 22, verses 21–35 |
| earth | Genesis chapter 1 |
| fish | Jonah chapters 1 and 2 |
| giant | 1 Samuel chapter 17, verses 38–51 |
| house | Luke chapter 10, verses 38–42 |
| ink | Galatians chapter 6, verse 11 |
| jail | Acts chapter 12, verses 1–11 |
| king | 1 Kings chapter 3, verses 5–12 |
| lion | Daniel chapter 6, verses 1–23 |
| manger | Luke chapter 2, verses 4–7 |
| needle | Acts chapter 9, verses 36–41 |
| oil | 2 Kings chapter 4, verses 1–7 |
| picnic | John chapter 6, verses 5–14 |
| queen | 1 Kings chapter 21, verses 1–16 |
| raven | 1 Kings chapter 17, verses 1–6 |
| shepherd | John chapter 10, verses 11–15 |
| tent | Genesis chapter 12, verses 1–8 |
| unleavened bread | Exodus chapter 13, verses 7–10 |
| vineyard | 1 Kings chapter 21, verses 1–2 |
| wall | Nehemiah chapters 1–6 |
| box | Exodus chapter 37, verses 1–9 |
| yoke | Job chapter 1 |
| Zion/ heaven | Revelation chapter 21, verses 18–27 |

# Also available from the Banner of Truth Trust

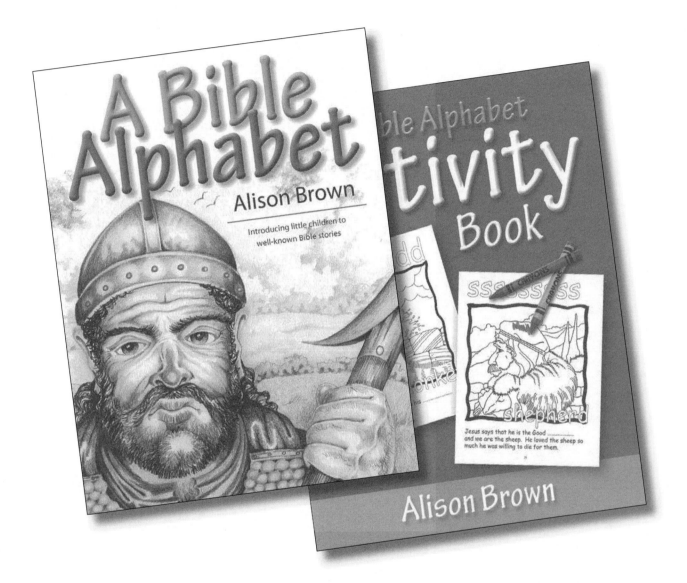

This *Bible Alphabet Activity Book* is based on another book by Alison Brown. *A Bible Alphabet* is a beautifully illustrated, full-colour book which introduces very young readers to some of the great stories and characters from the Bible, including Noah and the ark, David and Goliath, and Daniel in the lions' den.

ISBN 978-0-85151-963-0
large format paperback 32pp

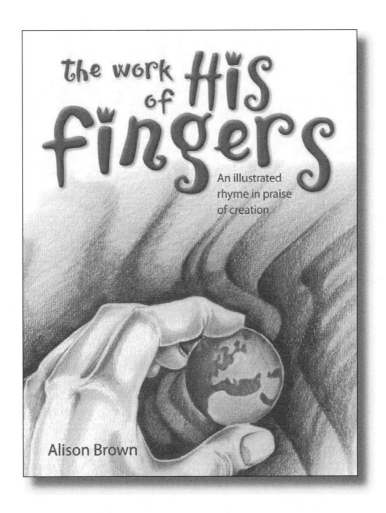

Alison Brown, a former primary school teacher, lives with her husband and five children in Co. Fermanagh, Northern Ireland. Alongside her love for drawing in both ink and coloured pencil, she takes great delight in turning the thoughts of children to the amazing truths of the Bible. Keeping in mind the kind of questions inquisitive children often ask about their world, she has written and illustrated this beautiful book which will help them think about the wonders of God's creation.

*When I consider your heavens, the work of your fingers, the moon and the stars, which you have ordained, what is man that you are mindful of him?*
Psalm 8:3-4.

ISBN 978-0-85151-965-4
large format paperback 32pp